CW00456604

Text: *Carl Rogers*

Photographs: *Carl Rogers, David Rogers, Shutterstock, Tony Bowerman, Centre for Alternative Technology*

Design: *Carl Rogers*

© *Carl Rogers 2017*

Carl Rogers has asserted his rights under the Copyright, Designs and Patents Act, 1988 to be identified as the author of this work. All rights reserved

This book contains mapping data licensed from the Ordnance Survey with the permission of the Controller of Her Majesty's Stationery Office.

© *Crown copyright 2014 All rights reserved. Licence number 100047867*

Ordnance Survey Licensed Mapping   **Partner**

ISBN 978-1-902512-28-0

A CIP catalogue record for this book is available from the British Library

Top 10 Walks series created by
Northern Eye Books

Northern Eye

www.northerneyebooks.co.uk
www.top10walks.co.uk

Cover: *Mynydd Mawr.* Photo: Carl Rogers

First published under licence from Northern Eye Books in 2017 by : **Mara Books**
22 Crosland Terrace, Helsby, Cheshire WA6 9LY
Email: carl@marabooks.co.uk

For sales enquiries, please call 01928 723 744

   Twitter: @CarlMarabooks
                                    @Northerneyeboo
                                    @Top10walks

Contents

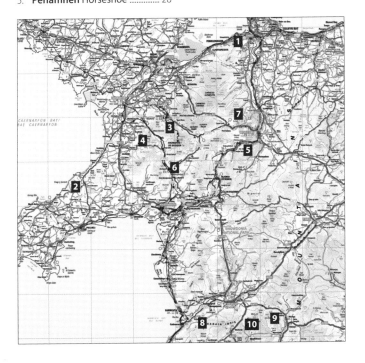

Snowdonia National Park

Snowdonia is one of the most celebrated and spectacular highland areas in the British Isles — a region of hills, lakes, mountains and wild moorland occupying the northwest corner of Wales.

Snowdonia National Park (Parc Cenedlaethol Eryri) was established in 1951 as the third National Park in Britain, following the Peak District and the Lake District. It covers 827 square miles (2,140 square kilometres) and, rather surprisingly, has 37 miles (60 kilometres) of coastline. There is great variety within this small area — the park contains all of Wales' 14 highest mountains, as well as a host of lakes, woods, beautiful valleys and high moorland.

The unique flora and fauna of the area includes rare mammals such as otter, polecat and feral goat. Birds of prey include peregrine, osprey, merlin and red kite, with rare plants like the Arctic-alpine Snowdon lily and the unique Snowdon hawkweed.

Snowdonia's hills

Snowdonia is famous for its rugged high ground rather than its softer green hills, but all great mountain areas are fringed by foothills and Snowdonia is no exception. These hills are every bit as diverse as their mountainous neighbours — from the shapely coastal hills of Llŷn and the moorland hills of the east, to the wooded hills of Dyffryn Conwy, the Dyfi Forest and the mini mountains of Mynydd Mawr and Tyrrau Mawr.

This lower ground is often neglected in favour of celebrities like Snowdon or the Glyder, but some superb days can be enjoyed on these lesser summits with half the effort, superb views, and you will often have these quieter hills to yourself.

"It's easier to go down a hill than up it,
    but the view is better at the top"

Henry Ward Beecher, *clergyman (1813–1887)*

Mynydd Mawr and Llyn Cwellyn

TOP 10 **Walks:** Hill Walks & Easy Summits

Snowdonia's lesser hills are generally not famous. This is not because they are of no interest, they are simply overshadowed by their giant neighbours. However, not all visitors have the time, energy or inclination required to spend all day on a tough mountain walk or scramble. This collection of walks on lower hills and easy summits is by no means a second best, but the very best half-day hill walks that Snowdonia has to offer.

Tal y Fan — page 8

Yr Eifl (The Rivals) — page 12

Moel Eilio group — page 18

Mynydd Mawr — page 24

Looking to the high Carneddau from Tal y Fan

Tal y Fan

A fairly easy walk along a broad ridge with superb views of mountain and coast

What to expect:

Good footpaths over heather moors and grassy fields. Rocky in places on the ridge

Distance/time: 8km/5 miles

Start: Drive through the village of Rowen and continue up the narrow lane for 1¾ miles to a T junction. Turn right and just after the lane swings left there is room for one or two cars on the verge

Grid ref: SH 731 714

Summits: Tal y Fan, Foel Lwyd

Ordnance Survey Map: Explorer OL17 *Snowdon & the Conwy Valley*

After the walk: Pub in Rowen

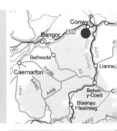

Walk outline

A steady walk from a high start point to gain the heathery, rounded Tal y Fan ridge where an out-and-back path takes you to summit of Foel Lwyd. The jaunt along the ridge to Tal y Fan summit is a delight in good weather with magnificent views across eastern Anglesey and along the coast to the Great Orme and beyond. A steep, grassy descent, followed by a good contouring path completes the round.

Tal y Fan

The name Tal y Fan means the 'place at the end', and describes it perfectly. This little hill is the northern-most summit in the Carneddau range, the 'place', at the 'end' of the mountains. Though modest in height, Tal y Fan is a prominent feature in views looking west across the northern Conwy Valley and you will be able to enjoy unrivalled views all the way along the ridge.

Maen Penddu standing stone

This northern edge of Snowdonia is littered with prehistoric remains. The walk passes a Bronze Age standing stone known as Maen Penddu and you will probably see several semi-wild Welsh mountain ponies that thrive on these open slopes.

Welsh mountain pony

The Walk

1. Walk back along the tarmac lane (the distance will depend on where you parked) to reach the **signed footpath** over the **wall** on the north side of the lane. A good path rises directly up through two rough grazing fields separated by a stone wall and crossed by a stile.

Just below the crest of the ridge, cross a **stile over the wall** on the right. Turn left up beside the wall at first, then veer half-right to the rounded crest of the ridge where another stile leads over the wall. Cross the stile.

2. To include **Foel Lwyd** (worth it for the views of the Carneddau) turn left along the broad ridge and follow the path beside the wall. Return to this point to continue.

For **Tal y Fan** turn right (ahead from Foel Lwyd) and follow the path along the ridge — a mix of grass, heather and rocks — with wide views on both sides.

The summit is marked by a triangulation pillar on the far side of the fence. Views take in eastern Anglesey, the Great Orme and northern Carneddau.

Continue to the eastern end of the ridge and, where the **wall** turns to the right and begins to drop, bear left down the northern slopes. Take one of the faint paths which drop into a small hollow where there is a **small stone enclosure** on the left. Continue ahead and soon you will be able to see to a small **fenced**

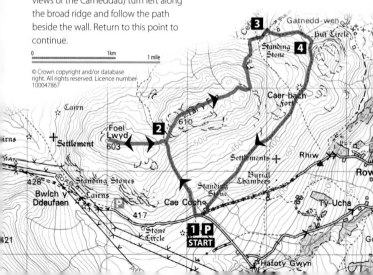

0   1km   1 mile

Grand view: *Tal y Fan offers superb views to the Carneddau, over to Anglesey and along the coast to Llandudno*

area of mine workings below. Pass the mines on their left-hand side to join an obvious track immediately below the spoil heap. Follow this track to a T junction with another track and turn right.

3. Shortly you pass a small Bronze Age standing stone, **Mean Penddu,** on the right. About 15 metres beyond the stone, and just before the track bends left, bear half-right off the track and aim for a large **metal gate** in the wall ahead. About 10-15 metres before the gate, bear left to walk beside a stream and soon you will pick up a reasonable path between stone walls. Stay by the left-hand wall until it opens out into a large field. Walk straight ahead through the centre of the field in the direction of a small pointed rocky summit ahead. In the bottom corner, go through a **gap in the wall** and walk ahead to eventually meet a grass track. Turn right along the track.

4. Follow the track, ignoring a left fork, soon with a ruined wall on the left. The path curves right beside a well-built wall and continues ahead. After a gate in a crossing wall the path continues ahead.

Eventually a **cottage (Cae Coch)** comes into view ahead. The path passes below the cottage and curves left to reach a **farm track**. Turn right along the track to reach the tarmac lane. Go ahead along the lane to complete the walk. ♦

Yr Eifl from Aberdesach

Yr Eifl (The Rivals)

A walk over two spectacular coastal hills with stunning views and some of the best Iron Age remains in Wales

What to expect:
A mix of good paths with rougher terrain between the two summits

Distance/time: 5km/3½ miles

Start: From Llanaelhaearn the B4417 rises steeply to 856 feet before dropping to the village of Llithfaen. Just beyond this high point, a lane bears to the left and a few cars may be parked on the verge

Grid ref: SH 367 434

Summits: Tre'r Ceiri, Garn Ganol

Ordnance Survey Map: Explorer 253 *Lleyn Peninsula West*

After the walk: Pub in Llithfaen

Walk outline

A straightforward ascent on good paths leads to the first summit with its incredible Iron Age remains. The link path between Tre'r Ceiri and Garn Ganol is less distinct and will require more careful route finding. Views from Garn Ganol are magnificent in clear weather particularly on clear evenings. Descent is on good paths over the easy-angled heathery western slopes of the hills.

Yr Eifl

The triple summits of Yr Eifl (often Anglicised to 'The Rivals') present a prominent and impressive skyline from almost anywhere on the Llŷn Peninsula, the west coast of Anglesey and even some of the western summits of Snowdonia. Seen across the blue waters of Caernarfon Bay or against a western sunset, their simple form is iconic. They are also almost unique in rising straight out of the sea, so every one of their modest 500 metres or so, is appreciated to the full.

A herd of feral goats are one of the more unusual residents of these hills.

Hut circles, Tre'r Ceiri

Feral goat

The Walk

1. Go through the old **iron kissing gate** opposite (on the north side of the road) and head directly up the sloping field towards **Caergribin**, a prominent castellated rock on the skyline. Higher up a ladder stile leads onto the open heather-covered hillside. As you approach Caergribin, the path curves left around the rocks.

The next objective, **Tre'r Ceiri**, can be clearly seen now rising to the northeast with its encircling walls. A narrow footpath leads through the heather, soon swinging left to join a more prominent path coming up from Llithfaen at a T junction. Turn right here and a little further on cross a **stone wall**

by a large ladder stile. As you approach the final slopes of Tre'r Ceiri keep left at a fork and make the final rise.

Enter the **stone enclosure** (remains of the hill fort) through the obvious entrance at the southwestern end just above the **information board** and make your way through the hut circles on the right-hand edge of the enclosure to the **summit**.

You will need little imagination to visualise the settlement as it was, the site is remarkably well preserved and this, along with its vast size may have given rise to the name — Tre'r Ceiri — which means 'town of the giants'.

Hilltop fortress: *The summit of Tre'r Ceiri is enclosed by some of the best preserved Iron Age remains in Britain*

The outer walls, some six feet thick and up to fifteen feet high, enclose an area almost 900 feet by 400 feet, and are composed entirely of dry-stone walling. Within this are the remains of some 150 hut circles of varying size and shape, all well preserved. Of particular note is the survival of the walls almost to their original height. A wall walk and parapet which enabled defenders to patrol the walls is also in amazingly good repair.

2. From the summit walk north (towards Caernarfon Bay) and bear left to walk beside the wall. Pass a **tunnelled exit** in the wall and continue to a second **paved entrance** above the saddle between Tre'r Ceiri and the main summit of Yr Eifl. Leave the enclosure here and bear right to exit through a **gap in the lower wall**. Turn right immediately and follow a faint footpath which soon curves left-wards through the heather with the summit of **Garn Ganol** directly ahead.

As the hillside becomes steeper, the path turns diagonally-leftwards,

'Bird's eye view': *Part of the magnificent panorama from Tre Ceiri*

eventually joining the main footpath that rises steeply from the left. (Alternatively, reach this point by returning to the stone wall crossed earlier and follow the main path that ascends the hillside to the right).

Turn right and make the short rise to the summit (Garn Ganol).

3. From the **triangulation pillar** a path descends southwest, initially between **two small ridges** of broken rocks, then through heather with the village of Llithfaen directly ahead. Lower down as

the angle begins to ease, cross the faint remains of a **dry-stone wall** running at right angles to the path (this is visible from higher up on the hillside). Turn left here and follow a narrow path which runs beside the stone wall with the green dome of Mynydd Garnguwch (the hill with the pimple-like cairn on its summit) rising directly ahead.

Keep ahead where the wall disappears and cross a path that leads down to a **cottage by pines** on the right. Further on you meet a track that also leads down to the cottage seen previously. The track forks here. Take the right-hand fork which is straight ahead as you

approach. This track shortly runs into fields where an **old iron ladder stile** crosses the fence by a gate. The right of way follows the edge of a depression or gully running through the centre of the field. Follow this and just before a wall corner, bear left, cross the gully and head across the field. Aim for a gate in the far fence that soon becomes visible. Continue through the following field to the kissing gate used earlier to complete the walk. ♦

Exiled King

Nant Gwrtheyrn is a secluded valley on the seaward side of Yr Eifl, traditionally held to be the final retreat of Vortigern, the exiled British king who lost control of his kingdom to the Saxons in the fifth century. His troubles arose as the result of an attempt to enlist the help of Saxon mercenaries to defend his kingdom from the Picts and Irish. Today Nant Gwrtheyrn is the location of a Welsh language centre.

Moel Eilio from Moel Cynghorion

Moel Eilio group

Superb walking over a group of high, grassy hills with unrivalled close-up views of Snowdon

What to expect:
Grassy, high-level paths, bridleways and lanes to start and finish

Distance/time: 11km/7 miles (14km/9 miles for longer option)

Start: There are a number of car parks in Llanberis. Start in the High Street where the side road, 'Capel Côch Road' is signed to the Youth Hostel.

Grid ref: SH 578 601

Summits: Moel Eilio, Foel Gron, Foel Goch & Moel Cynghorion

Ordnance Survey Map: Explorer OL17 *Snowdon & the Conwy Valley*

After the walk: Choice of pubs and cafés in Llanberis

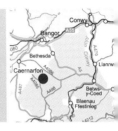

Walk outline

A rising lane leads from Llanberis onto the broad open moors above the town. This is followed by an easy-angled grassy ridge to the summit of Moel Eilio. The connecting ridge to Foel Gron and Foel Goch is a switchback high-level ridge with great views on all sides. An optional out-and-back to Moel Cynghorion is included (recommended in clear weather for the superb close-up views of Snowdon) Return to Llanberis is by old farm roads.

Moel Eilio group

These hills suffer from the proximity of their larger and more famous neighbour. However, they do provide an excellent ridge walk with superb views, particularly of Snowdon, and are often clear when the higher peaks wear a cap of cloud. You will also escape the crowds on these hills. To walk this lovely ridge in fine weather and have it more or less to yourself, is to enjoy Snowdonia at its best. The walking is easy underfoot and you can do it all in an unhurried half-day.

Snowdon up close

The wheatear loves the grassy tops, so keep your eyes open along the ridge and on the northern slopes of the mountain on the descent.

Wheatear

The Walk

1. Follow '**Capel Côch Road**' as it rises out of the village. Higher up the road changes name to '**Ceunant Street**' and eventually the houses and cottages are left behind. Pass the **Youth Hostel** on the left and continue to the lane end high above Llanberis.

There is a house on the left here ('**Hafod Uchaf**') and a gate ahead. Go through the gate and turn right at a T junction along a rough farm track to cross a stile beside a second gate. Continue along the stony track ahead passing under **overhead cables**, and about 50 metres before the next gate across the track, turn left onto a grassy path. This leads shortly to a stile beside a gateway in a wall. Cross the stile and keep following the path ahead.

The next section will take you up the steep, pathless slopes to the right to reach the crest of the ridge above. Choose your own line, it is all much the same. You need to leave the track by the time **Llyn Dwythwch** comes into view ahead at the latest.

2. Zig-zag steeply up to the rounded

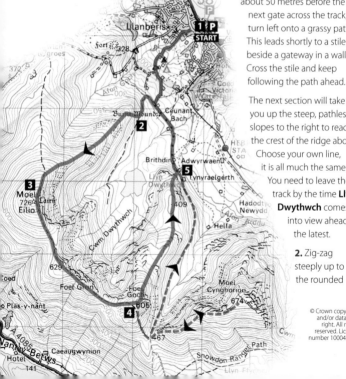

Big brother: *This walk gives superb, up-close views of Snowdon*

crest above. A **wall** and then **fence** runs directly up the ridge all the way to the summit, a steady 2 kilometre climb, a narrow but visible path all the way.

There are superb views all the way up this ridge, particularly to the left across Cwm Dwythwch and the northern ridges of Foel Goch and Moel Cynghorion to Snowdon.

The final section steepens a little as it merges with the broader and less interesting north ridge.

The **summit of Moel Eilio** *itself is broad, flat and grassy, the highest point marked by a surprisingly well-built stone wind shelter. The view takes in Snowdon, Moel Hebog, the shapely peaks of the Nantlle Ridge and Mynydd Mawr, along with the distant hills of Yr Eifl (The Rivals) on the Llŷn Peninsula. To the north, the Isle of Anglesey is laid out like a map, with the shapely summit of Elidir Fawr rising beyond Llanberis.*

3. A developing footpath follows the ridge in a southeasterly direction close to the broken cliffs that fall into **Cwm Dwythwch** and with Snowdon rising

Switchback ridge: *Looking back along the rolling green ridge from Moel Cynghorion to Foel Goch, Foel Gron and Moel Eilio*

ahead. Further on **Llyn Cwellyn** comes into view down in the valley to the right with the striking profile of **Mynydd Drws-y-coed** rising beyond.

Foel Gron is little more than a slight rise on the ridge, the main climb of almost 100 metres taking you to the grassy top of **Foel Goch** (almost 2 kilometres from Meol Eilio).

(The ridge falls steeply beyond Foel Goch to **Bwlch Maesgwm** before rising to **Moel Cynghorion** and then on to Snowdon beyond. It is difficult to include Moel Cynghorion into a circular walk but if you are feeling energetic you could take an out-and-back walk along the ridge returning to the bwlch. From there take the broad path north to return to Llanberis.)

4. From Foel Goch the most interesting return route heads due north along the broad, easy-angled ridge where a faint path follows the **fence**. About halfway down the ridge the fence swings left, but the path continues ahead crossing a **stream** to eventually reach a stile. Cross the stile and continue on a narrow but visible footpath taking a contouring line with a **wall** down to the left and

Llyn Dwythwch below you in the valley. Continue to reach a stile beside a gate in the wall on the left. Cross the stile and bear right, soon by a **fence**, to make a short steep descent to a **farm track** that can be seen below.

5. Turn left and follow the track back to the lane-end used at the start of the walk. Go through the gate on the right here and follow the lane back to Llanberis to complete the walk. ♦

Glacier footprint

From the summit of Moel Cynghorion you can see directly into the rocky mountain hollow below the huge cliff face of Clogwyn dur' Arddu. This was carved by a small glacier in a late glacial period and its 'footprint' can be seen clearly from here. Look for the mound of stones and earth protruding from the cwm. This is a moraine — a bank of debris pushed forward by the glacier marking its maximum extent.

Mynydd Mawr and Foel Rudd rising above Llyn Cwellyn

Mynydd Mawr

An excellent mini mountain walk with grand views into Nantlle and across to the famous Nantlle Ridge

Distance/time: 10.5km / 6½ miles.

Start: Begin in the village of Rhyd-Ddu on the A4085 Caernarfon to Beddgelert road. There are paying car parks for Snowdon immediately south of the village.

Grid ref: SH 569 530

Summits: Foel Rudd & Mynydd Mawr

Ordnance Survey Map: Explorer OL17 *Snowdon & the Conwy Valley*

After the walk: Pub at Rhyd-Ddu

Walk outline

Easy walking on forest tracks to access a sweeping grassy ridge which is followed to the sub-summit of Foel Rudd and finally Mynydd Mawr. Views into Nantlle across the crags of Craig y Bera are magnificent. Descent is made by Afon Gôch, rocky in its lower section, to the shores of Llyn Cwellyn, with a lakeside return along forest tracks.

Mynydd Mawr

Mynydd Mawr is one of those hills that suffers from its close proximity to Snowdon. Standing barely chest high to its giant neighbour, the vast majority of visitors turn their backs on it and head in the opposite direction. But this great little hill is certainly not without interest. It has an impressive craggy southern face rising above Dyffryn Nantlle, a huge castle-like north face rearing up above Llyn Cwellyn, narrow grassy ridges and the hidden valley of Cwm Planwydd. All are visited on this lovely route starting in the village of Rhyd-Ddu.

Keep an eye open for the formidable peregrine, which nest on Mynydd Mawr's high, inaccessible crags.

Mynydd Mawr summit

Peregrine

The Walk

1. From the '**Cwellyn Arms**' in the centre of **Rhyd-Ddu** (junction of the A4085 and B4418) take the **B4418 Nantlle road**. In about 150 metres, turn right onto a forest road immediately after '**Cefn Cwellyn**'. Follow the forest road for just over 1km/¾ mile before bearing left on a signed footpath that climbs to a stile on the edge of the woods.

2. Cross the stile and turn right along the forest edge following the crest of the ridge. At the end of the trees, climb the steepening grassy ridge ahead to gain the subsidiary **summit of Foel Rudd**.

Follow the easy-angled connecting ridge westwards from **Foel Rudd** passing along the crest of **Craig y Bera** with dramatic views down the shattered crags to the pastures of Nantlle below.

Soon the path veers right-wards away from the cliffs to make an easy rise to the rounded summit of **Mynydd Mawr** with its superb views to Snowdon and south to the famous Nantlle Ridge.

3. Return can be made via the ascent route, but a more interesting circular walk with more of an exploratory feel can be made by returning to the crest of **Craig y Bera**, then bearing left down easy angled, but initially pathless heather slopes, with occasional scree, to join a faint path on the left bank of **Afon Gôch**.

Lower down, just before the angle steepens and you can see **Llyn Cwellyn** below, cross over to the right bank of the stream. This avoids difficult ground where the stream cascades into a small **ravine**

Grand view: *Looking across Nantlle to the serrated outline of the famous Nantlle Ridge*

beneath the dark dripping crags of **Castell Cidwm** (*'Castle of the Wolf'*).

4. Below the ravine and waterfall, and just before woods, cross the stream again. Make your way between rocks and young pines to cross a stone wall

in the corner by a **rock face** on the left. Walk down to the shore of **Llyn Cwellyn**.

Just before the water turn right on a path to a gate that continues to pass a small **quarry** on the right. Soon, join a forest track and follow it to the road (A4085). Turn right and follow the road back to Rhyd-Ddu to complete the walk. ♦

Mountain or hill?

The name Mynydd Mawr translates as 'great' or 'big mountain', yet its modest height suggests a hill rather than a mountain. In this case the 'great' or 'big' refers to the bulky nature of Mynydd Mawr rather than its height. Another name for this hill was 'Elephant Mountain' — again a reference to its bulky form rather than its height.

Looking back to Y Ro Wen

Penamnen Horseshoe

A high grassy ridge walk with superb views of central Snowdonia. Pathless in places with very few visitors

What to expect:
Farm tracks and high, open moors, pathless and boggy in places. Steep descent

Distance/time: 14.5km/9 miles

Start: Dolwyddelan. There is a free car park beside the railway station near the village centre

Grid ref: SH 738 522

Summits: Y Ro Wen, Foel Fras & Mynydd Penamnen

Ordnance Survey Map: Explorer OL17 *Snowdon & the Conwy Valley*

After the walk: Pub in Dolwyddelen

Walk outline

A long but easy climb on rough farm roads gets you onto the rounded ridge at the first summit, Y Ro Wen. This is followed by mainly level walking around the rim of Cwm Penamnen taking in the summits of Foel Fras and Moel Penamnen, the high point of the walk. The long grassy east ridge of the mountain and steep woodland paths lead back to Dolwyddelan.

Penamnen Horseshoe

The group of grassy hills that enclose Cwm Penamnen are little gems. Lying in a secluded corner of central Snowdonia they seem to attract little attention and, having walked this route several times I have never once encountered another walker. Tackling this group in a horseshoe walk is a pleasing option, keeping you high once you have reached the first summit and enabling you to enjoy grand views into the Cwm Penamnen and to the impressive skylines of both northern and south Snowdonia.

Y Ro Wen summit

Keep a look out for red kites, which can occasionally be seen this far north and enjoy the vast displays of the silky cotton grass swaying in the breeze on the numerous high-level bogs.

Cotton grass

The Walk

1. Turn left out of the car park, cross the **railway bridge** and at the T junction turn left along '**High Street**'. Soon the lane begins to climb and at the end of a **stone terrace** on the right, turns left. Don't follow the lane here, instead go ahead along an access road with the stream to the right. After a house on the left, the right of way continues as a footpath that rises steadily beside the **stream**.

Higher up, the footpath joins a **farm track** that continues the climb up onto the higher pastures with widening views back to Dolwyddelan, Moel Siabod and the distant Snowdon group.

Stay with the farm track all the way to the **summit of Y Ro Wen**, about 3.5km/2¼ miles.

Despite the intrusion of the farm track, this summit feels quite remote, its central position giving it a 360 degree panorama of hills, moors and mountains. The higher tops of northern Snowdonia all lie to the north across Glyn Lledr, with Moel Siabod

The roof of Wales: *The view north from Moel Penamnen to Snowdon*

being the most prominent. The striking outlines of the Moelwynion lie out to the west with the Rhiong and Arenig hills to the south. To the east and the southeast lie the vast moors of the Migneint.

2. From Y Ro Wen a narrow path heads southwest beside the remains of an **old fence** on the left at first, then, where this veers away, trends right-wards to run close to the **pine plantations** which mark the rim of the **Cwm Penamnen** to the right.

Continue along the forest edge passing a stile on the right leading into the trees.

(You could use this path to cut the route short if needed. It heads down through the forest to join the road in the bottom of the valley.)

This path follows the line of the Roman road known as Sarn Helen. It gained the ridge here having crossed Afon Lledr at Pont-y-Pant and ascended the steep headwall of Cwm Penamnen. From here it continued south to the fort near Trawsfynydd (see the box on P33).

3. Continue ahead close by the woods

Mountain panorama: *There are superb views into the mountainous heart of Snowdonia for much of this walk*

on the right at first, then begin to veer away left as you approach **Foel Fras**, a minor summit ahead. This is little more than a small rise on the plateau-like moor and you are left to guess at the highest point.

Moel Penamnen can be seen ahead in clear conditions, but it is easy, in poor visibility, to mistakenly continue beside the fence.

Break away from the fence at the edge of the forest and head west where

paths soon become visible again along the gentle ridge to Moel Penamnen, a surprisingly attractive little summit with grand views to Moelwyn Bach and Moelwyn Mawr and down to the quarries of Blaenau Ffestiniog.

Like the previous summit, Moel Penamnen is a confusing place in poor visibility and even in clear weather the route is not always obvious.

4. From the **summit** a visible grassy path heads north for about 300 metres, then swings northeast to a **stile in the fence** at GR 718 489. Cross the stile and go ahead (northeast) along the broad rounded ridge.

At the edge of **conifer plantations** bear left parallel with them.

5. In about 1km/¾ mile you reach a broad, **grassy saddle** with a signed footpath into the **trees** on your right.

Follow this path down through the **plantations** to the lane in the bottom of Cwm Penamnen. Follow the lane left out of the valley back to **Dolwyddelan** to complete the walk. ♦

Sarn Helen

Sarn Helen, the Roman road running almost the entire length of Wales (connecting Aberconwy in the north with Carmarthen in southwest Wales), climbs out of the Glyn Lledr through Cwm Penamnen to reach the saddle between Y Ro We and Foel Fras crossed on this walk. It then continued south to the fort at Trawsfynydd. It is thought to have been named after the Celtic saint, Elen of Caernarfon.

Looking towards Bwlch-y-Sygun with Moel Siabod in the distance

Mynydd Sygun

Steep and sometimes stony walking to two magnificent little summits with some of the best views in Snowdonia

What to expect:
Steep, stony paths with some boggy sections. Paths generally good

Distance/time: 8.5km/5¼ miles

Start: There a large pay and display car park in Beddgelert near to the Tourist Information Centre. Start the walk from the Prince Llewellyn pub by the stone bridge in the village centre.

Grid ref: SH 590 481

Summits: Mynydd Sygun, Moel y Dyniewyd

Ordnance Survey Map: Explorer OL17, *Snowdon & the Conwy Valley*

After the walk: Pub and Cafés in Beddgelert

Walk outline

From Beddgelert a steep climb of almost 300 metres takes you high above the village to Mynydd Sygun, a high point on a rolling heathery plateau. Easier walking with great views to Snowdon takes you to the slightly higher Moel y Dyniewyd. The return leg takes you down to the shores of the pretty Llyn Dinas with a straightforward riverside return to Beddgelert.

Mynydd Sygun and Beddgelert

This modest little hill stands high above the village of Beddgelert and offers unrivalled views of both Nant Colwyn and Nant Gwynant, as well as some of the most shapely summits in Snowdonia. Mynydd Sygun and the adjacent Moel y Dyniewyd stand as high points on a rolling plateau of heather, rocks and desolate grassy cwms. It is perfect walking country: once the climb is over you can explore with ease and take in the magnificent views.

Beddgelert

If you see a small brown bird, it is likely to be a meadow pipit. They are common and widespread in hilly grassland habitants such as this.

Meadow pipit

The Walk

1. From the **Prince Llewellyn** pub in the centre of Beddgelert, cross the **stone bridge** over the river and turn left immediately. Follow a short access road that ends at the public toilets and coninue ahead crossing the **footbridge** over **Afon Glaslyn**.

2. Cross the footbridge over the river and take the path ahead (ignore the left fork by the river) heading for the righthand end of a **brightly coloured terrace**. Turn left along a road at the end of the terrace and in a few metres take the signed footpath on the right. The path heads up a **driveway** and onto the open hillside between **two cottages**.

The path is rocky and, climbing steeply, takes you high above Beddgelert to reach a **grassy shoulder** with views ahead to the shapely peaks Yr Aran and Y Lliwedd, both part of the Snowdon group.

Turn right and continue the climb, less steeply now, on the stony path to eventually reach a **kissing gate** in a stone wall. Go through the gate and bear right continuing the climb more gently.

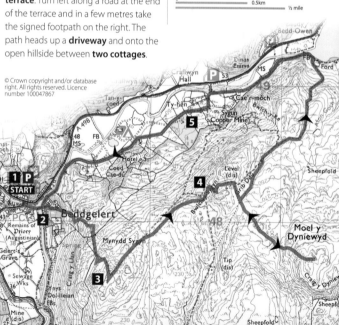

A view of giants: *Superb view of the Snowdon group from Mynydd Sygun*

The summit of **Mynydd Sygyn** is a broad heathery plateau with numerous small tops. The highest point is marked by a stone cairn and is easy to identify in clear conditions.

At just 300 metres Mynydd Sygun stands knee high to lofty Snowdon, yet it offers some of the best views in northern Snowdonia.

3. From the summit cairn head south — in the direction of Cnicht — to join a good crossing path a few metres lower down. Turn left along this path and follow it along the broad heathery ridge in the direction of the distant cone of Moel Siabod and the shapely top of **Crib Ddu** nearer at hand. The path is well-used and easy to follow.

Pass a group of **small pools** and an area of flat rocks, and a little further on there is a short **scramble over rocks** with a grassy hollow down to the right.

Immediately before the rise to Crib Ddu, a cairn marks **Bwlch-y-Sygun** where paths cross the ridge.

Mountain vista: *A panorama from the modest summit of Mynydd Sygun, with the Snowdon group (left), Moel Siabod (centre) and Cnicht and the Moelwynnion (right).*

4. Keep ahead here shortly reaching a hollow of grass and rocks. Ignore a path to the right, taking the path ahead zig-zaging up past a **large finger of rock**. Cross a stile over the fence and pass through an area of **rust-coloured mining spoil** to reach a junction of paths.

For **Moel y Dyniewyd** turn right here and immediately before a stile over the fence, take the narrow path left. This keeps close to the fence on the right.

Just before the highest point, cross a ladder stile on the right to reach the **summit**. Retrace your steps back to the path junction to continue.

Turn right signed to '**Llyn Dinas**' and follow the well-constructed footpath down to the **lake**.

Turn left by the outflow through a kissing gate and, ignoring the footbridge on the right, follow a good path ahead beside **Afon Glaslyn**. Pass a stone-built house on the left and eventually join the access road to **Sygyn Coppr Mine**.

Bear left with the road, and keep ahead ignoring the left fork to the car park.

Immediately after the road passes through a gap in the wall, turn right onto a footpath which runs beside the wall. The path eventually joins a narrow **tarmac lane**.

5. Turn left along the road and follow it along the valley floor passing a **camp site**. Immediately before the **bridge**, take the signed footpath on the left. Follow the riverside path back to Beddgelert to complete the walk. ♦

Sygun Copper Mine

Copper has been extracted from this site since the earliest times — first as surface excavations, then by means of tunnels when surface deposits were exhausted. The large caverns that can be visited today date from the Industrial Revolution, however, cheaper foreign imports in the mid 1800s made the mines less viable and they closed in 1903. Sygun Copper Mine was opened as a tourist attraction in 1986.

Crimpiau and Creigiau Gleision from Llyn Crafnant

Creigiau Gleision

A walk along a high spectacular ridge on the edge of the Carneddau with stunning views

What to expect:

Forest and high moorland paths, often muddy. Rocky in places

Distance/time: 12km/7½ miles

Start: Llyn Crafnant Forest Enterprises car park just before the lake. WC facilities are provided

Grid ref: SH 757 618

Summits: *Creigiaù Gleision, Craig Wen, Crimpiau*

Ordnance Survey Map: Explorer OL17, *Snowdon & the Conwy Valley*

After the walk: Tearoom by the lake, pubs & cafés, in Llanrwst

Walk outline

This route follows the skyline above the Crafnant valley giving spectacular views west towards the Glyderau, Ogwen and Snowdon, as well as Llyn Crafnant cradled in its wooded valley. The route through the conifer plantations as well as sections of the broad ridge can be very boggy. Footpaths improve after the main summit with a straightforward descent into the valley and return beside the lake. Views from the many summits on the ridge are some of the best in Snowdonia

Creigiau Gleision

Though little more than waist high to the Carneddau giants, Creigiau Gleision is arguably one of the best summits in the group, offering some of the most spectacular views in Snowdonia. The walk along the ridge has interest all the way. The panorama across the Ogwen valley to the rocky teeth of Tryfan, the Glyderau and Snowdon, as well as the fjord-like finger of Llyn Cowlyd a dizzying 300 metres below will rival anything the higher summits can offer.

This is an ideal place to see and hear ravens with their distinctive 'croaking' call.

Creigiau Gleision summit

Raven

The Walk

1. Turn right out of the car park and walk up the lane to **Llyn Crafnant**.

The lake and undulating skyline enclosing the valley make an attractive view and look more Lake District than Snowdonia.

2. Turn right crossing the **outflow stream**, through the gate and along the broad **forest track** that swings left just above the lake shore.

In about ½ mile/700 metres, bear right at a **fork**. This track climbs gently for another ½ mile or so before making a sharp right-hand **hairpin bend**. Just after the bend, take the signed footpath off the main track on the left. This is obvious at first but soon becomes a bit vague as it climbs quite steeply and directly up through the trees. One or two waymarkers keep you on the right path. The path becomes more obvious again higher up and after

swinging left-wards eventually merges into a broader forest track. Ignore a grassy left fork and look for a waymarked path on the left a little further on.

This path cuts off a large loop in the forest track meeting it again after a section that can be quite wet.

3. Cross the forest track and take the path opposite again. This continues the climb to eventually reach a stile out of the woods and onto the open moor.

Take the path directly ahead beside the scant remains of an **old fenceline** to reach the broad ridge crest at a large **marshy area** crossed by a fence.

Mountain view: *Looking towards Tryfan and the Ogwen Valley from Greigiau Gleision*

Ignore the ladder stile over the fence ahead, instead, turn left on a path parallel to the fence. Where the fence turns right and rises more steeply, cross by the remains of an old stile and follow the better path on the opposite side (fence now on your left). At the top of the rise, cross a **stile over the fence** in the corner and follow the obvious footpath swinging left-wards along the rounded knobbly ridge.

At the first summit you are greeted in clear conditions by a breathtaking view down to Llyn Cowlyd and across to Pen Llithrig y Wrach and the distant blade of Tryfan.

Continue along the ridge over the rocky **eastern top** to the main summit of **Creigiau Gleision**.

4. Make a short, steep rocky descent from the summit to a large, flat grassy area followed by a slight rise to the first of many small rocky tops. From here drop more steeply to a smaller flat area or saddle. The path keeps to the right of the next rocky top (**Moel Ddefaid**)

Surprise view: *The stunning panorma from the summit comes as quite a surprise!*

The views from the ridge have been magnificent all the way from Creigiau Gleision but are even better from here!

followed by another steep descent to a large **flat marshy area** occupying the next saddle.

Keep to the right of the marshy area and the large rocky summit that follows (**Craig Wen**). Walk over the shoulder of Craig Wen and descend to **stone walls**. Go through a gaps in the walls, and follow the path down to the next **saddle**. Take the path ahead, which bears half-right at first, then curves left-wards to rise more directly to the final summit of **Crimpiau**.

5. From Crimpiau take the obvious path east to join the **Capel Curig/Llyn Crafnant path** at its highest point.

Turn left along this path (ignore a right fork almost immediately) and follow the obvious path down into the Crafnant valley.

Lower down, cross a **stile beside a gateway** in a wall and bear half-right through a small open field to join a **lane** by a gate. Don't go through the **gate** and along the lane ahead, instead, take

the second track on the left here (first left leads to 'Blaen-y-Nant' farm). Pass **two houses** on the left and immediately before the gate to '**Hendre**' turn right over a **footbridge**. A well made footpath skirts the house through an area of **young pines** then continues close to the shore of the lake.

At the end of the lake turn left down the lane to return to the forest car park. ♦

Lakes and reservoirs

This ridge separates two of the largest lakes in the area: Llyn Crafnat to the south and Llyn Cowlyd to the north. Llyn Crafnant is famed as one Snowdonia's prettiest lakes. Its name means 'valley of garlic' from 'craf' and 'nant'. Llyn Cowlyd by contrast is a beak, dark stretch of water, its claim to fame being is its depth — at 229 feet (70 metres) it is the deepest lake in North Wales, although its depth has been increased by the building of two dams.

Tyrrau Mawr and Llyn Cyri

Tyrrau Mawr

A wild and stunning walk over one of the satellite summits of Cader Idris with amazing views over Cardigan Bay

What to expect:
Quiet lanes, 4x4 tracks and grassy hill paths, some vague and boggy in wet conditions

Distance/time: 18.75km/11¾ miles

Start: There is a sizable car park at Llynnau Cregennen reached by narrow lanes from Dolgellau.

Grid ref: SH 657 143

Summits: Craig-y-llyn & Tyrrau Mawr

Ordnance Survey Map: Explorer OL23 *Cader Idris & Llyn Tegid*

After the walk: Nearby Llyn Gwernan Hotel

Walk outline

Quiet lanes and ancient trackways lead onto the western end of Cadair's great north-facing escarpment. This is followed by easy walking along a high, undulating grassy ridge with spectacular views in all directions. Descent is by the upper section of Cadair's Tŷ Nant Path with a return along lanes.

Tyrrau Mawr

Lakes and mountains go hand-in-hand and are essential elements in any classic highland view — think the Snowdon Horseshoe from Llynnau Mymbyr, Scafell and Great Gable from Wastwater.

The view of Cadair Idris' northern cliffs seen against a foreground of Llynnau Cregennen is perhaps the classic mountain view in southern Snowdonia. In this view the main summit is not Cadair Idris as many think, but Tyrrau Mawr, little more than a minor rise on Cadair's long west ridge. A minor rise it may be, but combined with the Craig-y-llyn ridge, Tyrrau Mawr provides an excellent hill day with some of the best views in Snowdonia.

These quiet hills are an ideal habitat for the upland fox.

Prehistoric standing stone

Fox

The Walk

1. Turn right out of the car park and walk along the lane to the T junction. Turn right again and follow the narrow lane past the large ruined house of **'Hafotty-fach'** on the right.

Where the lane forks a little further on, bear left onto a **lane** signed as 'unsuitable for motors'. Very soon the tarmac disappears and the lane continues as a **rough 4x4 road**.

2. As the road begins to rise a **standing stone** can be seen over to the right.

It is worth the short detour for the view from the stone — the impressive backdrop provided by Tyrrau Mawr and the wide sweep of the southern Arenig and Rhinog hills beyond the Mawddach.

Follow the rising track to a **small saddle** where it levels before contouring the hillside with wide views right-wards to the resort of Barmouth and up the Ardudwy coast towards the graceful hills of the Llŷn Peninsula on the skyline.

Continue on the contouring track to a broad shoulder where there are **conifer plantations** on both the right and the left. Continue ahead a little further ignoring a signed footpath on the right to the first of two signed footpaths on the left. This is just before the end of the conifer woods on the right.

Sea view: *The view from Tyrrau Mawr over the Mawddach estuary to Cardigan Bay with the hills of the Lleyn Peninsula in the distance*

3. Turn sharp left and follow the visible footpath that runs parallel to woods over to the left.

Higher up the summit of **Craig-y-llyn** comes into view. Aim for this and you will eventually reach a **stile at a junction of three fences** (GR 649 113). Cross the stile and head directly across the following grazing field to a second stile overlooking the drop into the broad cwm cradling **Llyn Cyri** with a superb

view along the Craig-y-llyn ridge to **Tyrrau Mawr** — perhaps the finest view to be had of the hill.

4. Cross the stile and follow the **steepening ridge** to the western top (named as 'Twll yr Ogof' on the OS map) where you will get your first view to **Penygadair** — the highest summit on Cadair Idris.

The walk along this ridge is a delight in clear conditions — almost level with wide views in every direction and the feeling of height far greater than its modest 600 metres (just under 2,000ft) would suggest.

Mountain pool: *Craig-y-llyn and Tyrrau Mawr enclose the secluded Llyn Cyri*

Beyond Craig-y-llyn the ridge drops to a broad saddle with a final grassy rise to **Tyrrau Mawr**, its summit perched on the very edge of the mountain's 450-metre north face.

Tyrrau Mawr means the 'great towers'— probably a reference to the shattered rocks of hill's northern face. Seen from Llynnau Cregennen, Tyrrau Mawr looks almost as impressive as Cadair Idris and makes a fine backdrop in any view of the lakes.

The summit can come as a bit of an anticlimax, being so overshadowed by

Penygadair. However, you can enjoy the same amazing view out over Cardigan Bay to the distant Llŷn Peninsula

5. Footpaths lead on either side of the fence almost due east to the saddle at **Rhiw Gwredydd** from where the upper section of the **Tŷ Nant Path** continues the climb to Penygadair and there is a junction of paths.

Go through the gate on the left and head down the Tŷ Nant Path, surfaced with **stone steps** in the upper steep section. Lower down the path runs beside **a stone wall** to a point where **three walls** meet.

Don't go through the gate ahead here (continuation of the Tŷ Nant Path) go over the **stile** on the left a few metres back and follow the obvious footpath down through grazing fields. After the second wall the path **zig-zags** down to meet the narrow lane used earlier to reach Llynnau Cregennen. Turn left and the car park is an unavoidable 3.5km/2¼ miles along the lane. ♦

Crash site

The metal plaque close to the path on the slopes of Craig Cwm-llwyd commemorates the crash of a US Flying Fortress that hit the hillside in poor visibility on the first leg of its flight back to America on 8th June 1945. Trying to steer a course from Northamptonshire to RAF Valley on Anglesey in low cloud the pilot took a fatal inland course. All ten of the crew and the ten passengers also on board were killed on impact.

Maesglase (Maen Du) and Ty'n-y-braich farm

Maesglase

An impressive walk on a little-know hill hidden in the folds of the Dyfi hills. Views are superb

Distance/time: 12km/8 miles

Start: Car park in Dinas Mawddwy on the outskirts of the village on the lane heading northeast just before the bridge

Grid ref: SH 860 150

Summits: Maen Du

Ordnance Survey Map: Explorer OL23 *Cader Idris & Llyn Tegid*

After the walk: Pub in Dinas Mawddwy

Walk outline

Easy walking from Dinas Mawddwy into the impressive cwm cradled by the sweeping grassy crests of Maesglase and focused by the impressive crags at the headwall with the silver thread of its nameless waterfall. After a stiff pull onto the shoulder of the hill, the going is easier with stunning views from the rim of the crags beside the falls. Descent is by the steep northeast ridge followed by a gentle return to Dinas Mawddwy.

Maesglase

Maesglase is best seen from the east on the A470 between Dinas Mawddwy and Bwlch Oerddrws where its fine eastern flanks are buttressed by sweeping grassy ridges. These contrast starkly with the dark brooding crags rising at the head of a beautiful, green valley all but hidden from the highway. You will also be delighted and no doubt surprised by the nameless waterfall that cascades over 150 metres to the valley floor.

Red kites are increasingly common in southern Snowdonia and love the secluded corners of these hills.

What to expect:

Easy low-level paths followed by steep, grassy hill paths. Care needed on the descent

Un-named waterfall

Red kite

The Walk

1. Turn right out of the car park and walk along the lane out of the village. Cross the **bridge** and turn left immediately down the access road to a **caravan site**. In a few metres bear right on the signed footpath that rises diagonally up to a field gate. Follow the path ahead, soon rising to a small gate into an old **green lane**. Follow the lane left — little more than a footpath here — as it contours below **woods**.

2. Beyond a **cottage** down to the left, the lane becomes surfaced and swings left to cross the **river** (ignore a right turn before the bridge). Rise to a T junction and keep left to the main road (**A470**). Turn right and soon cross over to take the narrow lane opposite.

Follow the lane past a **farm** and continue as it rises gently.

As the lane levels Maesglase comes into view along with the impressive waterfall at the head of the valley.

A little further on, just before the lane starts to descend, take the signed footpath into fields on the left. The right of way follows a faint farm track as

Secluded valley: *Looking up to the valley head below Maesglase*

it makes its way to the head of the cwm eventually passing **woods** on the left. There are some modest **mine ruins** just before the final steep climb to **Blwlch Siglen**.

The view back into the valley backed by the lofty Aran Fawddwy peeping over the rounded shoulder of Glasgwm and Y Gribin, is striking and a fore gleam of things to come. The view south is across the wooded, lower hills of the Dyfi Forest to the wind farms of Mynydd Cemais.

3. Turn right up beside the **woods** on the left, steeply at first, then more gently as the path veers right towards the edge of the **crags** seen earlier.

As you approach the top of the **waterfall** the path nears the edge of the alarmingly steep slope (take care here especially in wet or windy conditions). The going is easy, but a careless step could be nasty. You will see a small **rocky pinnacle** ahead with a stream to its left. Cross the stream here and admire the dizzying cliffs below. Anyone brave enough can climb onto the pinnacle

Dizzy heights: *'Dare Devils' can climb the rock pinnacle above the waterfall for a spectacular view into the valley*

for an even better view of the water tumbling out of sight on its 150-metre fall to the screes below.

The going is much easier now as the path continues around the rim of the cwm to what appears to be the **summit of Maesglase**. In fact the highest point (debatable, see box) is another 400 metres to the northwest (marked 'Maen Du' on the Ordnance Survey map) but it is worth descending a few meters to admire the narrow grass ridge that sweeps down to **Ty'n-y-braich** farm.

The summit is almost an anticlimax after the excitement above the waterfall and is marked only by a fence crossed by a stile. The view is superb though, taking in the Rhinog hills to the north, the Arans to the east, Cadair Idris to the west and the vast plateau of mid Wales to the south. The western top is a simple out and back jaunt with even better views to Cadair Idris. Again there is nothing to mark the summit.

4. The map shows a zig-zag path down the northern slopes below the eastern top that swings back east to join the ridge after about 100 metres, but there is little sign of this on the ground. The only visible path descends steeply

beside the **fence** heading northeast from the summit. This is very steep at first but you are soon on the broad **saddle**. A faint path continues over the crest ahead but it is better to take the permissive path **which** can be seen heading diagonally-right. This path leads easily down to **Ty'n-y-celyn** farm and along the access track to the **A470**. Turn right and retrace the outward journey to complete the walk. ♦

Missing summit?

Despite its striking outline from the valley, the precise location of the highest point on Maesglase seems to be the subject of some confusion. Traditionally, the top of Maen Du (674 metres at SH 823 152) was regarded as the summit. However, more recent surveys suggest that the top of Craig Rhiw-erch (c 676 metres at SH 817 150, some 600 metres to the west) could be higher, thus making it the true summit.

Mynydd Ceiswyn

Ratgoed Horseshoe

*A rolling ridge of secluded hills with great views hidden
amongst the woods of the Dyfi Forest*

What to expect:

*Steep forest paths/tracks
and grassy ridge paths.
Some boggy sections*

Distance/time: 15.25km/9½ miles
Start: Follow the minor lane which leads from the A487 to
Aberllefenni. Continue through the village passing the Mountain
Centre in about 500m. Shortly after this the lane bends sharp left
and there is a layby on the bend where a few cars can be parked
Grid ref: SH 777 101
Summits: Mynydd Ceiswyn, Waun-oer, Cribin Fawr, & Craig Portas
Ordnance Survey Map: Explorer OL23 *Cader Idris & Llyn Tegid*
After the walk: Pub in Corris

Walk outline

*Initially easy walking on forest roads then a steep climb
through woods to a high, broad ridge crest with wide views.
This is followed by a leisurely jaunt along the ridge over the
summits of Waun-oer and Cribin Fawr. Return is made by the
sweeping grass edge of Mynydd Dolgoed forming an excellent
horseshoe walk.*

Waun-oer and Cribin Fawr

These hills lie hidden amongst the woods of the Dyfi
Forest. Overshadowed by both Cadair Idris to the west and
the high Aran ridge to the northeast, and with no striking
outlines to catch the eye, they are rarely visited. But once
you are out of the woods and onto the ridge you can
enjoy a long elevated walk with minimal effort over several
summits and with superb views to the rugged peaks of
Cadair Idris and the contrasting wooded ridges of the Dyfi
Forest.

On Cribin Fawr

The colourful, carnivorous sundew thrive in the boggy
upland hollows. They lure and digest insects to supplement
the poor mineral nutrition of the soil in which the plants
grow.

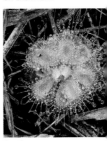

Sundew

the **river** and past **slate spoil** on the far bank. A little further on the track forks — the right fork crosses the river and heads off up the valley clear of the woods and the left fork goes back into the trees. Take the left fork.

Follow the broad **forest road** for over 1km/¾ mile passing two tracks on the right leading down to farms.

Shortly after the second track, look for a **signed footpath** on the left which heads diagonally up through the trees. The path climbs steadily for 2km/1¼ miles crossing other tracks on the way and giving only brief glimpses down into valley.

2. The path emerges from the woods just a few metres from the **fence** which

The Walk

1. Go right along the lane from the layby and shortly after the bend bear left onto a **forestry road**. Follow the road above

Wooded hills: *Waun-oer and Cribin Fawr from Mynydd Dolgoed*

straddles the broad grass ridge on the shoulder of **Mynydd Ceiswyn**.

There is a stile here and in clear conditions you will enjoy superb views to Mynydd Moel and Gau Craig on Cadair Idris. Behind is an impressive 400m fall into Cwm Ratgoed with the wooded ridges of the Dyfi Forest beyond. Off to the right you will see Craig Portas and the grass ridge of Mynydd Dolgoed at the head of the cwm that provide the second arm of the horseshoe walk.

Don't cross the stile, instead turn right and follow the footpath beside the fence. The ridge is easy and almost level to Waun-oer and you can stride out and enjoy the superb situation and contrasting views on either side.

3. Waun-oer is marked by a triangulation pillar and at 670 metres is the highest point on the ridge. The continuation to Cribin Fawr requires a short descent and climb at the only narrow point along the ridge.

The summit of **Cribin Fawr** is unmarked lying just to the north of the fence

Wooded ridge: *The sweeping wooded ridge of Waun-oer with Cader Idris behind*

---

junction where there are two stiles. The continuation goes along the right fence here so if you go in search of the highest point (100m or so away) return here to continue.

Stay by the **fence** heading southwest to a flat grassy saddle below the short rise to **Craig Portas**.

It is worth a short detour to the left here for the striking view into the valley and the sweeping slopes which rise to the northeast face of Cribin Fawr.

If you are collecting summits you will want to make the short climb to Craig Portas, otherwise bear right on a contouring footpath to crest the grassy edge of **Mynydd Dolgoed**. Like the Waun-oer ridge, this provides easy, elevated walking with superb views down into Cwm Ratgoed and across to Waun-oer with Cadair Idris peeping over the ridge.

4. Follow the ridge to its western end and descend beside the fence with woods to the left. Lower down the slope steepens considerably and you enter an **open oak wood**. Continue down until you reach a stile in the fence on

the left. Don't cross this, instead, head diagonally-right down through the trees to a **ruin** at the bottom of the slope. Walk ahead across grazing fields to reach a **track**. Turn left along this, passing a large house (**Ratgoed Hall**).

Continue for about 1km/¾ mile to cross the river at the fork visited earlier. Return along the forest road to complete the walk. ◆

Centre for Alternative Technology

Centre for Alternative Technology (CAT)

Founded in 1973, the Centre for Alternative Technology is dedicated to demonstrating and teaching sustainable development. Occupying a seven-acre site in the disused Llwyngwern slate quarry near Corris, it offers a visitor centre with hands on displays, a range of courses and publishes information on renewable energy, sustainable architecture, organic farming, gardening and sustainable living. For more info: www.cat.org.uk

Useful Information

Visit Wales

The Visit Wales website covers everything from accommodation and events to attractions and adventure. For information on the area covered by this book, see: **www.visitwales.co.uk**

Snowdonia National Park

The Snowdonia National Park website also has information on things to see and do, plus maps, webcams and news. **www.snowdonia-npa.gov.uk**

Tourist Information Centres

The main TICs provide free information on everything from accommodation and travel to what's on and walking advice.

Betws-y-coed	01690 710426	TIC.BYC@eryri-npa.gov.uk
Beddgelert	01766 890615	TIC.Beddgelert@eryri-npa.gov.uk
Harlech	01766 780658	TIC.Harlech@eryri-npa.gov.uk
Dolgellau	01341 422888	TIC.Dolgellau@eryri-npa.gov.uk
Aberdyfi	01654 767321	TIC.Aberdyfi@eryri-npa.gov.uk

Emergencies

Snowdonia is covered by volunteer mountain rescue teams. In a real emergency:

1. Make a note of your location (with OS grid reference, if possible); the name, age and sex of the casualty; their injuries; how many people are in the group; and your mobile phone number.

2. Call 999 or 112 and ask for the North Wales police, and then for Mountain Rescue.

3. Give them your prepared details.

4. Do NOT change position until contacted by the mountain rescue team.

Weather

The Met Office operates a 24 hour online weather forecast

Follow the link from the National Park website **www.eryri-npa.gov.uk/visiting/your-weather-forecast-service** or see www.metoffice.gov.uk